SECRETS OF SUCCESSFUL WRITERS

By

Othello Bach

CHOICE BOOKS

ISBN-10: 1500771775

ISBN-13: 978-1500771775

Printed in the United States of America

DEDICATED TO

Steve Haberman

Other Books by Othello Bach

Fiction
Simon Sees
Tainted
House of Secrets
Satan's Daughters
Rail Fever
Trapped
Brimstone Brethren
The Sacrifice
The Taking of Joanna

Nonfiction
Cry Into the Wind
How to Write a Great Story Teacher's Guide
Lose Weight with Hypnosis
101 Questions for God
The Father Within
Grow Your Self
Secrets of Successful Writers
Angel Within

Children's
Albert and the Monster
Whoever Heard of a Fird
Snigglefuzzle
Does My Room Come Alive at Night
Hector McSnector and the Mail Order Christmas Witch
How to Write a Great Story
Jake Snake's Race
Lilly, Willy and the Mail Order Witch
Monica's Hanukkah House
Snyder Spider's Birthday Surprise
The Biggest Sneeze
The Man With Big Ears
The Golden Slippers
Shermit the Hermit

TABLE OF CONTENTS

INTRODUCTION	7
FOREWARD	8
BEFORE YOU WRITE	10
Read & Research	10
Self-Publishing Online	11
What To Write	11
Training	12
Tone	13
Outline	15
Point Of View	17
Third Person	18
IT ALL BEGINS WITH A SENTENCE	20
Avoiding Overused Verbs	21
See It, Feel It, Write It	21
Use Exciting Verbs	22
Sentence Length	24
Sentence Structure	25
Learn By Modeling	26
Formula Fiction	27
Breaking Down The Formula	28
USE A TABLE	30
Genre Specific Information	30
Where Do You Get Ideas	31
Theme	33
WRITING THE STORY	34
Three Parts Of A Story	34
PLOTTING	36
PLOT DIAGRAM	39
White Elephant Problem	43
CHARACTERIZATION	45
Show It Don't Tell It	46

Faking Emotion   **48**
Character Motivation   **50**
Making Your Characters Believable   **52**
Creating Memorable Characters   **53**
Making The Unbelievable Believable   **54**
Different Thoughts And Emotions   **55**
Consistency   **56**
Quirks   **56**
Physical Environment   **57**
DIALOGUE   **60**
Blend Dialogue With Narrative And Action   **60**
Writing "Natural" Dialogue   **62**
Taglines   **64**
Show Action, Don't Tell It   **66**
Flashbacks & Transitions   **67**
AFTER WRITING   **71**
Setting Up A Manuscript   **72**
Query Letter   **73**
SALES AND REJECTIONS   **75**
ABOUT THE AUTHOR   **77**

INTRODUCTION

A great story is one that keeps your imagination racing and your eyes glued to the page. It keeps you turning pages to see what happens next, and when you finish the book the characters linger in your mind like old friends.

Every successful story has interesting and believable characters, a strong, exciting plot, natural-sounding dialogue and plenty of action to keep the story moving. But no one is born a great writer. Just as it takes years of practice to become an outstanding athlete, dancer, or concert pianist, it takes years of practice to become a great writer. However, if you enjoy using your imagination, the years of practice will go by quickly and will be worth the time and effort. As you work, you'll discover that the creative process adds new dimension to your own life. The art of bringing fictional characters and places to life, and making them so real that others can see and know them as well they know their own families, is both thrilling and deeply satisfying.

By the time you finish your first novel you will have suffered your characters' pain, delighted in their joys, felt their resentments and grieved their defeats and losses. You will have built their town or city, decorated their homes, made their breakfast and beds, and even slept with them. You will have robbed their banks, prosecuted the innocent, burned their houses, attended their churches and fornicated with the preacher's wife. But you will have also arrested the bank robbers, defended the innocent, help rebuild their houses—and perhaps even walk away with the preacher's wife.

If you take the time to make your characters real and give them a well thought-out plot to live through, you are the writer, director, producer, set designer, stagehand, and all of the actors of a production that others will applaud for years to come.

Trust me; it's worth it.

FOREWORD

There are two ways to learn any craft successfully: (1) trial and error, and (2) instruction.

Trial and error, undoubtedly, is the most time consuming, inefficient and frustrating method. The frustration frequently becomes so intense that would-be writers often become discouraged and suddenly have neither the time nor patience to continue. Reluctantly, they abandon their pursuit and suffer the stigma of failure when in reality they might have been only moments away from success.

Writers, perhaps more than any other single group, attempt to master their craft through the agonizing trial and error method. The reason for this is probably because many beginning writers naively approach their goal of becoming published authors. They believe that because they have insight, imagination, and a love for words and expression of thought, their stories should be published for millions to read and enjoy. How incredible! These same people would never expect a musician or an athlete achieve fame and fortune without specialized instruction.

"But creativity can't be taught!" people exclaim. And although this statement is true, what many of these same people fail to realize is that the rules - the do's and don'ts behind a professionally structured piece of writing – can be taught and must be learned if they want to sell their material.

These rules - the do's and don'ts of the craft - are the secrets, so to speak, that this handbook reveals. I have delineated what I believe to be the most important rules, tips, secrets - call them what you like - behind creative fiction writing. They are time-proven canons which unlock the mysteries of creative fiction so that you will not have to endure the tortures of trial and error learning.

When you have absorbed the contents of this unique manual,

you will be able to couple your creative and imaginative mind with the time-tested techniques of the craft that writers must follow if they are to become successful authors.

BEFORE YOU WRITE

There is but one absolute regarding fiction writing and it is this: there are no absolutes.

But there are general rules—do's and don'ts—which must be employed by new writers if they are to become skillful enough to one day abandon them.

For every suggestion and accepted "norm" mentioned in this, or any other book on writing, exceptions can be found in bestsellers or magazine short stories all the time. But that is not to say that the authors of these books and stories didn't know and at one time practice the rules; and in fact, that their material might have been better if the rules had been followed.

Established writers, already known for their excellence, can break rules with impunity; beginners can't.

Read and Research

Before you write the first word of a story, you should have some knowledge of which publishers are most likely to buy your story. In other words, find a market for your idea before you write it. You can do this by browsing online publishers' sites or studying reference books such as Writer's Market and Jeff Herman's Guide to Literary Markets, but be sure you are working from the latest publication. This research will make you reasonably certain of which publishers might want your story. Otherwise, you may have a great story idea, but it may not meet any of the current market needs.

For instance, you may write a perfectly wonderful and moving story about a shy little 40-year-old farm woman who wins a cake baking contest—the dream of her life!—and although you are sure every person in the world would enjoy your story (and perhaps you're right!), it is still a fact that there are many magazines that wouldn't touch it.

The reason is simple: some magazines want only stories about women who live in cities. Others want stories that show women in business situations, while still others want only stories about relationships.

Study the market. Become familiar with the publications and the publishers who publish the kind of books or stories you like to write. Otherwise, it will be hit and miss (and usually miss) all of your writing years.

Self-Publishing Online

Todays' writers have far more freedom than writers have ever had. The Internet allows anyone to publish almost anything. For some writers, it's simply a matter of "being published." Concern that the work is well constructed means nothing to them. If the last statement describes you, you need not read further. If, however, you want to be a successful writer who gains the respect of readers around the world, you may want to continue reading.

What to Write

Always write about something that interests you. What kind of stories do you like to read? Do you like mysteries or love stories? Perhaps you like science fiction or westerns. Whatever it is, that's the kind of story you should write. Read what you like to write and write what you like to read. Don't try to write about a subject or lifestyle unfamiliar to you because it will be all too obvious to an editor, or reader. If you must write about an unfamiliar lifestyle, be prepared to research until you have enough information and "feel" for the subject to be convincing.

If you aren't a reader of magazines, then you're not likely to sell stories to them. Use online resources to determine what the magazine wants, then study its format, style, and the nature of the stories it publishes.

There are books which can be purchased or checked out of the library that also contain information about the writing market. However, they must be current to be of value. Be sure that the one you use for research is the latest issue because editors and publishers change frequently and so do their needs.

When to Write

Beginning writers frequently read interviews with well-known authors and conclude that they should follow the same writing schedule as the successful writer. Drawing this conclusion is about as sensible as believing that because a prosperous businessman dictates letters at 3 p.m. each day, the only way to become a successful businessman is to write letters at 3 p.m.

Obviously, you want to write when you are most creative. For some people, it's as early as 4 a.m. For others, it may be as late as midnight. It doesn't matter when you write as long as you write regularly. Try to set a time each day and work for at least an hour. Spending less time will almost assure you of the slowest progress possible.

Training

Can a beginning writer who is not blessed with natural writing talent still become a successful writer? The answer, most emphatically, is YES!

Those who are sensitive to the needs and feelings of others and are willing to apply themselves to the task can become successful writers. It takes a lot of hard work, but even "talented" writers have to work hard.

Those who have been told they have a natural talent for writing often believe that all it will take to achieve fame and fortune is to quickly read through a "how to write" book. That's about as intelligent as a jogger deciding to workout at the local YMCA for a couple of hours in order to compete in the Olympics.

Training is as important to writers as it is to athletes. You must learn to think in descriptive phrases and sentences. No one naturally thinks in that way. You must teach yourself to think that way. For instance, we rarely think "I must remember to bring home a loaf of bread." Instead, our brain sends instant messages that make us recall that we must stop on the way home from work to buy bread. Then, we may verbalize that message: "Oh! Bread. I almost forgot."

So one of the training exercises a writer must do is to actually think in complete, descriptive sentences as often as possible. One way to practice is to take advantage of things you see and hear daily and put your impressions into complete sentences.

For instance, when you see a particularly interesting tree bent over from the wind, you can take advantage of that moment and describe the tree (in thought) as you might read aloud a line of prose: "The wind-beaten tree leaned like an old woman too weary to stand straight."

If a car speeds past you, your brain will make a mental note, but your conscious "writer's mind" must slow down to describe the car and sensation. In this way you teach yourself to create "on the spot" when you sit down to write. Then the awareness that *a car sped past me* becomes "The blue sedan whipped around me from the left and roared down the road, throwing a cloud of dust back against my windshield."

Seize every opportunity to practice and develop your ability to describe people and events.

Tone

The tone of a story is defined as the attitude toward the written material. It can be humorous, serious, erudite, bitter, romantic, nostalgic, fantasy, feminine or masculine. Every writer does one better than the others, but you will never know which you do best unless you try the various tones in a storyline. The tone of the story can change every aspect of your writing from the dialogue to character motivation.

It's expected that a horror story or thriller will open with, or soon develop, a dark and foreboding tone. The tone of any story is often set in the first line or two.

Example: *A gentle breeze brushed through the yard and sent autumn leaves tumbling playfully around her bare feet.*

OR...

A harsh, restless wind swirled through the yard and flung brown, dead leaves against her bare feet.

Generally, the scene sets the tone, but not always. There are funeral scenes in comedies as well as dramas, romances and horror stories.

If the preceding examples were the opening of a story, it's easy to see how different the stories might be.

The tone of dialogue is often assumed by the reader unless you inform them differently.

Example: *Doting mother to her child: "Want to help me?"*

Irritated co-worker: "Want to help me?"

Flirting construction worker to pretty girl: "Want to help me?"

Readers also bring their expectations to what they read. Unless you inform them otherwise, they will stereotype the characters. Your character may speak the same words but readers will assume the tone and read it according.

Outline

Not enough can be said for outlines. They are the road maps that guide you from one scene to another in a coherent, believable way without letting you wander aimlessly, and boring the editor. (Note that I did not say boring the reader. The reason is simple. Your story will never reach the reader if it bores the editor.)

You wouldn't be foolish enough to set out on a trip across unknown terrain in a foreign country without using a map or guide to help you reach your destination. Similarly, each new story idea is like an uncharted sea and you are likely to get lost if you work without a map ... or outline.

The outline can be as simple as you want to make it, as long as it helps you. A short story outline may take no more than half a page (certainly no more than a full page), while an outline of a novel could take several pages.

Remember, the principal reason for outlining is to guide you smoothly across an uncharted sea of situations, problems and complications. It is a must for coherent, well-structured writing.

The following is an outline of a fairly gruesome short story. Please note that it outlines only the action scenes, both the mental and physical action.

Outline of Story "Fair Exchange"

1) Young boy, Jeff, is jealous of his younger brother, Craig, who is a paralyzed and can neither speak nor move. The jealousy is prompted by parents' doting over Craig and ignoring Jeff.

2) Jeff begs to go live with an aunt and uncle who are fond of him, but parents refuse.

3) Jeff gets interested in witchcraft when a magazine article is brought to his class.

   a) He begins collecting things he believes necessary for his "altar" which includes a hawk's skull.

4) For several nights he tries to make Satan appear. Finally one night the hawk's eyes glow and he knows he's succeeded.

   a) He then tries to transfer himself into his brother's body and forces Craig into his body.

5) The magic works but the incantations and screaming bring his parents into the room. The son they believe is Jeff tells them, "No, I'm Craig."

   a) Later, Jeff transfers back into his own body.

6) Parents are worried and the next day Jeff hears them discussing the strange occurrence, but their main fear is what may be happening to Craig.

7) Jealousy peaked now, Jeff repeats the transfer of bodies the next night. Again, inhuman sounds bring parents into room. Again their "healthy" son screams at them, "Stop calling me Jeff. I'm Craig!"

8) Feeling powerful, Jeff repeats the transfer again the next evening, but this time, while he is now in Craig's body, the parents rush in and remove the son they think is Jeff.

a) From inside the room, confined within Craig's immovable, mute body, Jeff hears his parents send Craig away to live with his aunt and uncle.

9) When everyone has gone, parents come into Craig's room and try to console him, saying they're sorry "Jeff" upset him.

10) Unable to speak or move, Jeff, now locked forever inside Craig's body, is doomed in his own private horror chamber.

Point of View (or who tells the story)

Before you begin to write, decide which character can best tell your story. Generally, it's the one who is involved in the most action and who must solve the plot problem. Where there's action and empathy, there is also reader interest.

There seems to be a great deal of confusion between instructors and writers over the terminology used to describe the various points-of-view from which a story can be told. Rather than add to the confusion, I will suggest, simply, different ways a story can be told.

First Person

The personal "I" and "me" of this point of view have a confidential tone and are often used for romance and confession stories. However, it is restrictive. It limits your character's ability to know what is happening in any place other than where the narrator is. With this POV your character may observe, imagine, assume and conclude but cannot "know" anything except what is observed through the five senses as far as the other characters are concerned.

Example: *I couldn't believe he would say that to me!*

Third Person Limited

This POV uses the pronouns "he" and "she" but is still limited to one point of view, generally the protagonist's. You still aren't into their thoughts but you are seeing everything as they see it. It's more like watching a movie with the camera following the protagonist.

Example: *She couldn't believe he would say that to her.*

Third Person Omniscient

From this all-knowing point of view, you can delve into each character's thoughts and feelings—but not in the same sentence or paragraph. The writer must take one scene at a time to portray a character's thoughts but you cannot jump from one to another without giving warning to the reader. This warning may take the form of a transition line, a set or scene change, or by leaving several extra spaces between paragraphs. Extra space—two to four—in the manuscript let the reader know you are making a break with that scene or character.

- *Mable Kurtz heard a terrifying scream and saw something suddenly fall past her window. Rushing over to see, she searched the darkness below but saw nothing. She wished Artie were home; he would go down and find out what happened.*

- *Matthew's phone startled him awake. He grabbed it, but before he could wake up enough to think, George whispered breathlessly, "Matt! They killed Artie! Shoved him off the roof!"*

As you can see, each character must be handled separately in order to create emotional involvement you want from the reader.

Once you have determined whether to use a single or multiple points of view, the next task is to determine the best way to tell your story. Most fiction is written in Third Person, but it's up to you to know which will work best for you.

IT ALL BEGINS WITH A SENTENCE

Learning to write exciting, heartfelt and memorable stories begins at the beginning…the sentence.

A great sentence is one that forms a perfect picture in the mind of the reader. It does not have to be long and requires no special vocabulary. It merely communicates an idea so perfectly that the reader can see and feel it. Your goal is to create a mental picture for someone else to enjoy. You use words that you might never use in your daily or business communication. You express your thoughts in detail, being as clear and original as you can be.

A great fiction story is a series of pictures captured in words. It allows the reader to meet new characters and visit new places—all people and places that you have imagined and created for them. Perhaps the best part of fiction writing is that you, the writer, are in complete control of what happens in the world you create. You create the people, their families and homes, and every experience they have. You are the ruler of a tiny universe, where through your words others can visit and experience new and exciting situations.

You may write about a beggar or a rich man, and for the time that you are writing the story, you become that person. You think his thoughts and imagine all of his movements and words. The people in your tiny fiction universe must do what you want them to do, because you are the ruler... the writer who created them.

Avoiding Overused Verbs

Most unpublished writers have only one way to express their ideas. They use one or two verbs, and these tell the reader nothing. These two over-used verbs are *was* and *were*. While these words are fine if used *occasionally,* if used too often, they destroy an otherwise good story.

Example: *The sun was setting.*

While there is nothing wrong with that sentence, there is also nothing new or exciting about it. It tells the reader that it is early evening, but that's all. With just a little thought and effort, at least part of the sunset could be described so that the reader can see it. If the sunset is worth mentioning, then surely its beauty is worth sharing.

Example*: Long, golden fingers of light stretched across the evening sky and lingered there, as if pointing to tomorrow.*

Example*: Bill was fat. He was sitting in his chair, watching TV.*

Example*: When Bill sat in his recliner, the pillow of fat resting on his stomach almost blocked his view of the television.*

Example*: Sue was walking across the field when she fell down.*

Example: *Lost in her daydreams, Sue closed her eyes to enjoy the sunshine on her face. She walked with her face up-turned for several steps before she stumbled. Her legs gave way like a marionette whose strings had been cut.*

See it, Feel it, Write it.

Before you begin to write a sentence, imagine the scene you

want to paint with your words. Imagine you are the character you are writing about, and feel what that character feels. Smell what that character smells and hear with that character's hears. For an instant, before you begin to write, see and feel what you want the reader to see and feel.

Use Exciting Verbs

Bright pictures are painted with bright colors. Exciting stories are told with exciting verbs. Dull verbs such as *was* and *were* are weak and lifeless. Verb phrases such as *had been* and *have been* are even duller. The lack of life in these phrases is enough to kill almost any sentence.

Example: *It was almost dark. They had been walking for hours when they reached the farm.*

Why not paint a picture the reader can really see?

Example: *Darkness slowly overtook the valley as they trudged wearily up the road to the farm.*

Other dull verbs are: walk, talk, sit, stand and run.

Everyone walks, talks, sits and stands. To write, *he walked across the yard,* tells nothing about your character or his mood. There are many ways of walking, all of them more descriptive than *walk.* You might say, *he hurried, strode, trudged, sauntered, ambled, crept, sneaked, or jogged* across the yard. An alternative is to use adjectives to describe how your character walked. *He walked with slow and heavy steps.* Or... *She walked with a quick, light energy.*

You may also support weak verbs with adverbs: *He walked quickly. He walked slowly and heavily.* However, a strong verb is always better than the best adverb.

But the king of all dull, mindless, say-nothing verbs is the word *got*.

Example: *He got sick then she got up and got medicine for him. When he got out of bed she got his robe and got him outside right away. He got sick again. She was getting tired of him getting sick.*

Got is useless at conveying emotion. Look at how much more information the reader receives when action verbs replace the word *got*.

Example: *He fainted. She sprang up and grabbed his medicine. Awaking slowly, he pushed himself up. She draped his robe over his shoulders and then opened the door. They stepped outside. Immediately, he became ill again. She sighed, growing weary of his constant sickness.*

Verbs are action words. Choose verbs that show the action you have in mind for your character.

Rewrite the sentences below, using strong action verbs to replace the weak verbs in the sentences. At this point, avoid adverbs and adjectives.

Julie sat down and stared at Sam who stood in the doorway.

(Ask yourself *how* Julie sat. Was she prim and proper? Suggestive? Provocative? What kind of "stare" or expression did she have on her face? Then describe how Sam stood? Describe his posture and expression.)

Tammy walked over to see Tom. It was time to let him know why she was so angry. He saw her coming and looked away.

(*How* did Tammy walk? What was her expression and posture?

What did Tom's posture and expression say about him?)

Sentence Length

Words do more than paint pictures; they also create emotions within the reader. Carefully chosen words and well thought-out sentences can make the reader feel frightened, depressed, joyous, or heart-broken.

Even the length of a sentence helps to create a mood within the reader. Long sentences with several "ing" words slow down the pace of the story. Short sentences with strong, powerful verbs create a sense of action. Knowing this, you can actually slow the readers' minds and help them relax and enjoy the sunset that you painted with words. You can also speed up their minds and make them race when you want them to feel excited.

Example: Easing his head slowly onto the pillow, Jim marveled at how wonderful the bed felt beneath his tired, aching body. The pillow, caressing his head like a loving mother, comforted him as he allowed the exhausting tension to flow out of his arms, legs and back.

Or...

Example: Startled, Jim sprang up. The phone rang again. He fumbled for the receiver. It slipped from his hand and clattered to the floor. He grabbed it. "Yes? Yes?" He shook his head and tried to wake up.

If you are careful to select words that paint the exact picture you have in mind and you pay attention to the length of your sentences, the reader will love visiting your make-believe world.

Sentence Structure

Sentence structure defines the length and arrangement of the words in a sentence. Repetitive structure is monotonous and boring. To make a paragraph interesting, vary your approach to the ideas you are expressing. Instead of beginning each sentence with the subject (noun), open the sentence with a verb, adverb, or adjective phrase.

Example: *The bed was against one wall. The other wall had only a chair next to it, while a dresser stood in the middle of the floor. Nothing was on the fourth wall except a closet.*

In these similarly structured—and boring!—sentences, the reader learns nothing worth remembering. If the room is important enough to be in your story, take the time to paint a picture so that readers feel as if they are standing in the doorway looking at it. Do this by describing the items in the room and using strong verbs that help the reader see what you want them to see.

Example: *The shabby little room had only a few pieces of furniture. Without a window, the furnishings almost faded into the shadows. A small, unmade bed, its mattress sagging, squatted against the far wall. A tired, old chair and long dresser crouched humbly against the other walls, as if wanting to hide from the shame of their many scars and scratches. The open bottom drawers of the dresser suggested someone had emptied them in a hurry. The small, dark closet held nothing but a single warped hanger.*

Writing Exercise

Part 1 - Rewrite the sentences below using only five sentences. Describe these rooms so that readers will feel as if they have seen them.

There was a table in the room that had a book on it. There was a sofa, too. The end table held a vase of dead flowers.

The living room was small and cramped and there was far too much furniture in it. I bumped my shins twice just walking through it.

Part 2 – Describe two rooms that you've actually been in, and use enough detail that readers will feel as if they've seen them, too.

Learn by Modeling

One of the quickest ways to become a great writer is to study the writings of great writers. Working from a book that you enjoy reading, open it to one of your favorite paragraphs. Keep the book open so that you can look at that paragraph as you write. Then, using the paragraph as a guide, model your own paragraph after it. Rewrite each sentence carefully, changing words to make them fit your scene.

Example: *The sun warmed Helen as she skipped down the road to her grandmother's house. Little puffs of dust rose from the ground with every step she took. Her mind raced excitedly as she thought of going into town with her grandmother. Days of shopping with her were always fun.*

This is how you might rewrite it.

Example: *The rain poured down on John as he ran along the sidewalk to his aunt's apartment. Puddles splashed beneath his feet with every step. He dreaded days spent with his aunt. They were never any fun.*

By using a published paragraph as a pattern for what you might do, your writing improves. You are forced to describe the scene so that others can see it. However, because you have changed the characters and everything in the scene, the new scene is yours.

Writing Exercise

Part 1 - Using the following paragraph as a guide, rewrite it. Use the same sentence structure but change the details.

The elderly woman leaned heavily on her cane as she slowly made her way to the bus bench. She wore a floppy brimmed hat to shield her from the sun and a pair of sunglasses so big that they covered half of her face. She dropped to the bench as though she had taken her last step and never intended to move again.

Part 2 - Rewrite a paragraph from one of your favorite books. Use the same sentence structure but change the details. Make it completely new, completely yours.

Formula Fiction

Emerging writers often balk at the idea of writing formula fiction; they want to write a great American classic. I hope every writer reading this accomplishes that because we certainly need more outstanding, one-of-a-kind novels to read and reread for years to come. Unfortunately, accomplishing that feat is sort of like winning the lottery.

The dream of writing in complete freedom, without regard to rules and "norms" is just that—a dream. Most readers expect a certain amount of rules to be followed, and denying them the expected only leads to disappointment and a promise to never read your work again. So before you fall into that beguiling trap, remember that the best creations of the most famous artists who ever lived—Beethoven, Bach, and Michelangelo)—were all "works for hire." They followed the dictates of their employers. Their talents were used to compose, sculpt, and paint within the parameters set by their employers, primarily representatives of the Church.

Limits frequently draw out genius for the truly creative. Being the creative individual that you are, you, too, can create a masterpiece of fiction by "coloring within the lines."

Breaking Down the Formula

Just because you have a great idea doesn't mean it's salable. Every fast-food restaurant has its own version of a hamburger, but no two are exactly alike. All fiction stories have common elements but no two genres are the same. Knowing your genre is like knowing the recipe of the secret sauce for the world's best hamburger. Even then, of course, not everyone will agree that it's the world's best.

For instance, a gothic romance is similar, in places, to a suspense thriller. Westerns and adventure novels have similarities. Science fiction and fantasy have a few common features, but each is unique. The only way for a beginning writer to know exactly what is involved in writing a particular genre is to read that genre and learn the formula.

One way to learn the formula is to buy a book written about that particular genre. There are many, and you will probably find one to suit your needs. Most of them are written by writers who have published a number of books in that genre. Some books are extremely informative while others are about as helpful as reading a bus schedule, so spend a little time in a bookstore or library browsing for one that meets your needs.

Most publishers of genre fiction have writer's guidelines that they will send free of charge if you mail your request and include postage and a self-addressed envelope. Others post them on their web sites.

However, the best way to discover the formula of a particular genre is to do the research yourself. This requires more time, but in the process you will learn exactly what you need to know and you will never forget it.

Assuming that you have read several *recently published* novels similar to the one you want to write, let's also assume that you have copies of five or six of them to use for your research. You will also need three different colored markers to highlight certain sections.

Page through each book and highlight all the dialogue in one color then go back through and highlight the action scenes, and each complication or new problem in different colors.

This will take at least a couple of hours but it will be more profitable than a $1,000 seminar dedicated to that genre. By the time you complete this assignment you will know exactly what is expected in that kind of novel.

USE A TABLE

Genre Specific Information

Title	The Devil's Angel
Genre	Thriller
Publisher	Best Books
# of Characters	7
Characters' Gender	3 men, 4 women
POV	1st person, Female
Professional or Blue Collar	Professional
# of Complications	6
% of Action	35%
% of Dialogue	30%
# Subplots	2
Ending Up/Down	Up
# Pages	225

Following this example, gather genre specific information on each of the books you are using for your research. The highlighted areas will allow you to fill in the estimated percentages. A blank table has been included on the following page for your convenience. Make several copies of it, and use it until you are familiar with that genre.

Genre Specific Information

Title	
Genre	

Publisher	
# of Characters	
Characters' Gender	
POV	
Professional or Blue Collar	
# of Complications	
% of Action	
% of Dialogue	
# Subplots	
Ending Up/Down	
# Pages	

All of the information gathered is important because genre readers expect each book to contain specific elements. By compiling the information, you can easily see what is required for that specific genre. You will also know, at a glance, which publishers want "what" and how to fulfill their needs.

Soon you will begin to see a pattern developing, but don't jump to conclusions after two books and say, "Okay! I've got it!" Sometimes you will find enough variation to allow you more freedom than you originally thought. A few publishers may actually want something a little different.

By the time you've completed this research you'll know exactly what is expected of you from these publishers in that genre.

Where Do You Get Ideas?

This question is perhaps the most amazing of all questions regarding writing because ideas are everywhere. Newspapers are full of them. Everyone you know or meet will have a problem they are dealing with, so pay attention. A few minutes spent on a park bench observing others will prompt ideas. Overheard conversations... one line from a song... or a twist on an old story... all of these can balloon into wonderful story material.

Ideas are literally everywhere there is life – and sometimes where there's not. How many graveyard stories have you heard?

There are also gimmicks you can contrive for your convenience. Keep card files of possible characters and settings. Make a list of 10 different settings - desert, hospital, police station, drug store, mansion, mountains, etc., then make a list of 10 different characters - hillbilly, dentist, secretary, farmer, etc. Next, cut up your list so that each name and each setting is separate. Fold them all into neat little pieces, keeping the characters separate from the settings. Now draw one from each. You may have a dentist for a character and the mountains for a setting. Begin there. Why is the dentist there? Did his car break down? What if he is in a hurry to get to a convention still 10 miles down the road? What people might he encounter as he tries to hitch a ride? What if someone tries to rob him? What if his whole career is on the line if he doesn't attend the convention? What if ... what if ... until you have a story developing.

This is a forced way to create a story, but if you're really at a loss for ideas, you may want to try it.

Anytime you put a character in an unfamiliar setting a story will start to form. Many of the longest-running shows on TV have been built on this premise. Adventure is sure to take place if a city boy is lost in the country and vice versa.

Once you've decided your storyline, try giving your character a specific time limit in which to solve a problem. This creates suspense automatically and the problem will become more intense without any effort at all.

Although ideas are everywhere, you will rarely find a new one. However, there are original twists on old ideas, and this is exactly what is expected of each writer with each new story.

Theme

Every published piece has a theme or intense emotion or moral lesson that runs throughout the story. Some contain more than one theme, but this is generally not a good idea for a beginning writer. If you can condense your story idea into a one or two line theme, your chances of writing a salable story are greatly enhanced. By recognizing and identifying the theme, you can direct all of your narration, action and dialogue to reinforce, shape and define that theme.

WRITING THE STORY

Three Parts to a Story

There are three parts to a good story: (1) a beginning, (2) middle and (3) the ending.

A. In simple terms, your story must begin with a "hook," an opening statement that will grab and hold the reader's attention as you set the stage to reveal the protagonist's first problem. The "problem" might be a threat to the fulfillment of a lifelong goal or an unexpected event that prompts an immediate goal, such as a startling home invasion. Whatever the situation, it must be immediate, intense and all-consuming. You may or may not introduce the antagonist at this point, but you must provide evidence that one exists, as in learning of the kidnapping or rape of a loved one. While most protagonists are heroes, some are not. Dracula and Frankenstein are as popular as Superman.

B. Once interest has been established, you develop the body of your story with situations and complications that develop logically and build steadily toward a climax. The climax is the point in the story where the protagonist succeeds or fails ultimately in meeting the goal. If the protagonist fails, it is a tragedy. Most stories end happily with the protagonist succeeding at least partially. Happy endings are more popular than tragic endings, even in horror stories and doomsday science fiction, although both can be successful. This is achieved by making each successive scene more exciting or dramatic than the preceding one.

C. The final part of your story, the climax and ending must believably conclude to resolve the plot problem and explain the subplots that developed along the way.

Successful writers know that a good story always opens with a hook, builds with excitement, tension or suspense, and flows into a realistic climax, and then is quickly resolved. The ending of the story should not drag with numerous explanations. If the ending takes more than a couple of paragraphs for a short story or more than a couple of pages for a novel to conclude, then it probably will be an unsuccessful ending. Be specific. Don't generalize. Make your point and stop.

PLOTTING

Plotting is not only one of the most important elements of story writing, but is, perhaps, the easiest to learn because it can be "plotted" or charted. (See Fig. 1.)

There are several simple plotting rules that nearly all successful writers follow:

1) Every story, no matter how short or long, must begin with a problem. If your protagonist does not have a problem, there is no goal. The first problem, called the *inciting incident,* will set up more problems and conflicts as the protagonist attempts to reach his/her goal.

2) The protagonist must attempt to solve the problem realistically on his or her own. This means without divine intervention by means of a rabid bear charging out of the woods to eat the "bad guy," or any other unexpected hero—super or common—coming to the rescue.

3) The first problem-solving attempt will fail and the problem becomes more complicated and intense.

4) Once again, the protagonist must struggle to solve the problem, only to fail again and further complicate the problem. (At this point in a short story, the plot should reach its highest emotional/action level—or climax. The protagonist either succeeds or fails and the story problem is resolved immediately. In longer stories, such as novels, the complications and attempted solutions continue as necessary.)

Using the outline of "Fair Exchange" as an example, here's how a story would be plotted:

PROBLEM: Jeff is jealous of his parents' attention to his mute, invalid brother, Craig, and considers witchcraft as a possible solution.

ATTEMPTED SOLUTION: Fearful of using witchcraft, Jeff begs his parents to let him live with a favorite aunt and uncle.

COMPLICATION: Parents say he can't go and give even more attention to Craig.

ANOTHER ATTEMPTED SOLUTION: Jeff now turns to witchcraft and begs Satan to let him be transferred into his brother's body.

CLIMAX: His wish is granted and the transfer is a "success," but while Jeff is trapped in Craig's immobile body, the parents send Craig (whom they believe is Jeff) away to live with the favorite aunt and uncle.

Endings to stories can be uplifting, tragic or unresolved. Horror stories frequently use tragic or unhappy endings, the type of ending chosen for the story outlined above.

In this tragic ending, Jeff is trapped forever in a lifeless body while his parents spew a stream of sickening attention over him, all the while saying they are glad "Jeff" is gone as he was always such a thoughtless boy.

A happy or uplifting ending might have been for the parents to realize that Jeff had turned to witchcraft because he desperately needed their love, and they would have come to this realization just in the nick of time.

An "unresolved" ending would have been for the witchcraft experiment to fail and the story would remain as it began, with Jeff still jealous of Craig and his parents not understanding why.

Popular market magazines—whether online or paper—are specific in the type story endings they prefer. A quick reading of several magazines in each category - horror, romance, women's magazines, adventure, etc., will give a clear indication of which type stories and endings the various editors want.

With novels, there's considerably more freedom. The story simply must be well-plotted and the ending resolved satisfactorily.

PLOT DIAGRAM

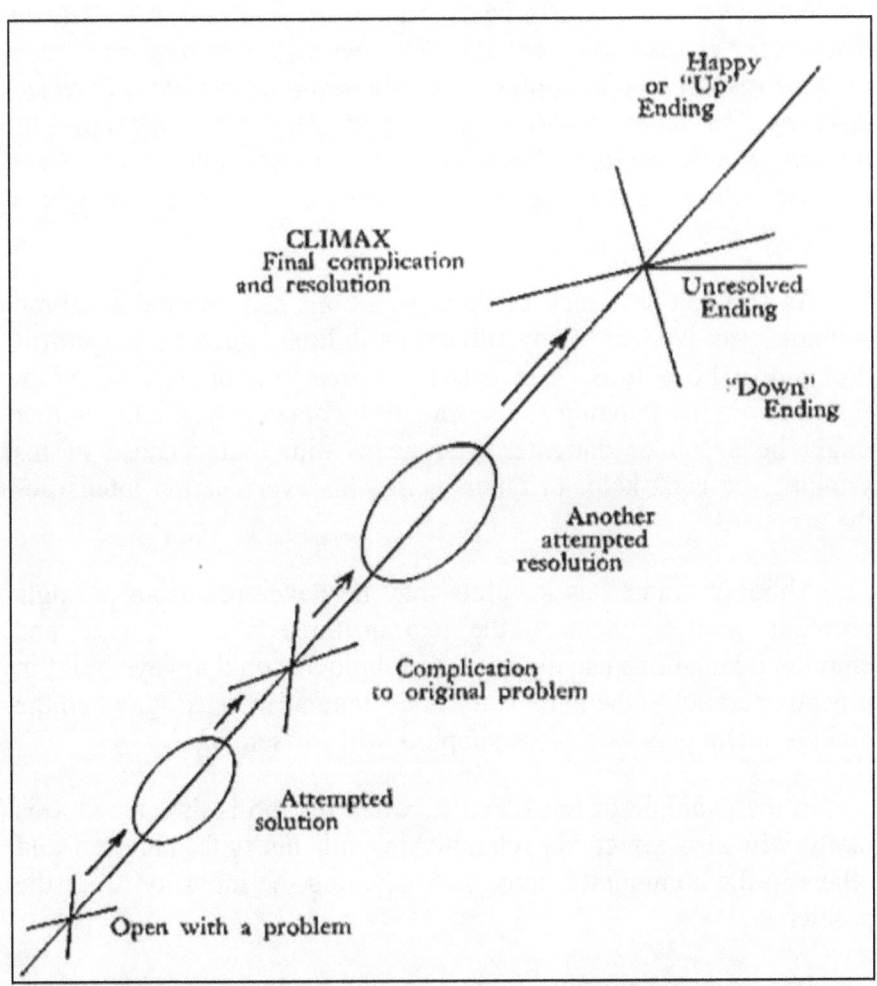

This diagram illustrates the simplest short-story plot. Depending on the length of the story, the attempts to resolve a problem and the number of complications can be increased as necessary.

Subplots

Successful subplots are the natural spin-off problems arising from the original problem.

Example: A brilliant scientist with many internationally known discoveries is also an alcoholic. The main plot is that he's been granted research money to develop a vaccine to combat a dreaded disease. The main problem likely will be focused on how he mismanages the research funds. He is also is likely to endanger lives because data is distorted in order to keep his drinking problem from being exposed.

As you can see, each of these situations can become a natural subplot... as well as many other possibilities, such as a spin-off problem of how drinking affects his marriage... or how he might fight to hold his standing in the scientific community... still another might be a son or daughter who needs him, but because of his drinking, he can't help. In other words, his every action intensifies the problem.

Although numerous subplots may be developed from a single problem, limiting them to the two or three most dramatic and emotional situations usually is best. Subplots should always build in urgency parallel to the main story line. Generally speaking, when the main problem gets worse, the subplots will worsen, too.

In the example of the scientist, when his job is threatened, this likely will also affect his relationship with his wife, children and others in the community, thus, strengthening the intensity of all the problems.

Too many subplots and your story will begins to read like a soap opera because there are too many transitions from one problem to the next. No one problem will surface as the central problem.

Subplots may be told from the protagonist's point of view or from many characters' points of view. They should be related to the main problem and resolved along with the main problem.

Endings (solving the problem)

Regardless of how convenient it would be to call in the Air Force or Marines to win a battle, the single soldier (your protagonist) must solve his own problems. In other words, if you write yourself into a corner and are forced to drag a bear from the woods to eat the bad guys, your story won't sell. If you self-publish such a weak story on the Internet, readers will probably skip your next story.

To avoid this mistake, think through the plot completely; chart it on the diagram to make certain it will work and be sure your protagonist is capable of solving the problem. If not, start again and this time either give the protagonist less of a problem or super human strength. YOUR PROTAGONIST MUST SOLVE HIS/HER OWN PROBLEMS!

Endings That Won't Sell

A convenient coincidence that miraculously occurs just at the most critical moment won't sell. It's not believable. It's acceptable to BEGIN a story with a coincidence, but not end with one.

Example: If a man abandons his job in an attempt to find a long lost brother, and the entire story deals with his obsession to locate his brother, it will not be believable that at the critical point of the story (after he finally loses his wife and home and is forced to move into a skid row flop-house) that he learns, by a wonderful coincidence, that his brother is sleeping on the next cot.

The editor (or reader) will be furious with you for having involved him in such an agonizing, heart-rending story, only to insult his intelligence at the end by solving the problem by coincidence.

Another commonly used, but unsalable ending is one where the hero or heroine struggles desperately throughout the entire story against certain impending doom, only to learn in the end that the source of fear was actually nothing to be afraid of at all!

Boo! Hiss! Everyone hates this kind of letdown. If you say there is a monster waiting to eat the good guys (unless they're smart enough to outwit or outrun it), there had better be a monster. If you write yourself into a corner and decide the only way out is to say: "But it was all a dream," don't be surprised if you get a few death threats.

There also is the "idiot plot," i.e. a plot built around the hero and heroine's apparent lack of intelligence. This occurs when the writer keeps trying to convince the reader that there is a big problem, yet the reader can perceive several solutions. A character that continually jumps to ridiculous conclusions is a common manifestation of the "idiot plot."

For instance, a woman hears on the radio that a man has been murdered across town and she immediately suspects her husband is guilty because he left the house without saying where he was going, and he had a "funny" look in his eye. Clearly, she appears to be an idiot. Then, if without further information to substantiate this ridiculous suspicion, she waits for her husband to come home then knocks him in the head with a skillet, ties him up, and calls the police - she isn't just an idiot, she's a total lunatic! Any fool can see that such a dim-witted character is creating her own problems, and no reader has time for such stupidity, or for an author who can't create a more believable problem.

To avoid the "idiot plot," make your characters smarter than idiots.

The plot cannot be a series of stupid happenings that any average person could solve with a moment's thought.

Contrived Situations

A borderline idiot plot is a story filled with contrivances—improbable situations that plague the protagonist as the story nears its climax. The intention is to create a greater sense of urgency, but because the situations are ridiculous last-minute contrivances, tension vanishes, instead. Sharp readers mock the silliness.

Example: The protagonist's daughter will be killed in one hour if he doesn't deliver the ransom that he struggled for half the story to get. He lives in the country and the drop location is 60 miles away. It is night (of course) and raining (of course.) He jumps into his old truck and takes off down a country road, slipping and sliding along the rough, muddy ruts. A little later, he's stopped by a tree which has fallen across the road. He jumps out, wrestles with the tree and finally shoves it over enough he can pass. In the process, his cell phone drops from his shirt pocket into the mud. He steps on it but doesn't notice. When he finally reaches the paved road leading into the city, an accident has traffic stopped. He desperately tries to find his phone. (Maybe he can buy some time.) Then he sees that he's about out of gas. Moaning and groaning, he abandons the truck and takes off on foot... and so on and so forth until readers begin to think this borderline idiot deserves to die. Even if he doesn't deserve it, the writer does.

Contrivances do not create urgency and suspense; they create irritation and homicidal impulses... within the reader... for the writer.

White Elephant Problem

This storyline involves a character that struggles valiantly to meet a goal, and gains it—then half way through realizes it is not what s/he wants—then s/he spends the last half of the story trying to get rid of it.

Example: A young woman struggles for 100 pages to become a nun. Through painful effort and sacrifice she succeeds, but soon she realizes that it is not the life for her. Now, her problem is to become a lay person once again without losing face and hurting all those people who worked so hard to help her to achieve her goal.

Keep in mind that if the goal is not worth achieving, it's not a good story problem.

Borrowed Trouble Problems

Avoid "borrowed trouble" plots. This problem-addict frequently disguises himself as a newspaper reporter who can't stand the boredom of his own life, so he pokes his nose into other people's troubles and takes on the battle of solving them.

While it has been acceptable in the past, today's readers are too sophisticated to believe that a big-hearted problem solver is going to intentionally risk his life just for a good headline.

So the rule of thumb on "borrowed trouble" is, simply: don't. The only acceptable circumstance is a husband-wife, parent-child or other close family relationship where the reader understands that the problem is critically important to the problem solver, or a detective who takes the risk for money. Otherwise, allow the character in trouble to solve his/her problems.

CHARACTERIZATION

There is no way to over-emphasize the value of good characterization.

A well-developed character is like a dear, beloved friend you will never forget. Yet, well-developed does not necessarily mean a character that is described physically from the crown of his cowlick to the hole in his shoe, unless such detail is important to your plot. The age, size and shape of your characters are not nearly as important as their emotions. However, there are times when your character's physical appearance plays a part in your story. When it does, take the time to describe the character so that readers feel as if they are looking at a photograph. Point out details that will create an emotional snapshot.

Example: *The large dark coat swallowed her, making it obvious that it was a hand-me-down.*

Or...

He tugged nervously at his shirtsleeves, self-conscious that they were too short.

Solid, believable characterizations are composed of emotional details that bring them to life and make them as real as your next door neighbor ... a person you care about or dislike. The reader can identify with their loves, hates and fears as deeply as their own. Clearly expressed emotional details give them substance and make heroes, friends or enemies out of otherwise ordinary "stick figure" characters.

The humanization of each of your characters will depend on your ability to develop them through a blend of narration, dialogue and action. None of these elements, however, can be utilized to create a solid character until you are able to recognize your own feelings, a trick that sounds complicated, but that is made simple merely by paying attention to yourself and being aware of your reactions to the five senses: sight, sound, touch, taste and smell.

For instance, does a strange sound frighten you or pique your curiosity?

What are your feelings when you touch something slimy?

Remembered sounds, odors and tastes can sometimes create a flood of emotion—some pleasant, some painful. Regardless of your reactions to the senses, if you pay attention and take time to describe what you're feeling, you will quickly sharpen your ability to describe your characters' reactions. Genuine emotion, expressed through your characters *becomes* your readers' experience. This is why they read; they want to live through a new, exciting experience—as someone else—but as someone as real as they are.

Show it. Don't *tell* it.

Show your characters' emotions instead of telling the reader how they feel.

Example: *Telling: Carla sat against the fence and cried during recess while the other kids ran across the schoolyard and played in the wind.*

Showing: Carla slumped against the fence like a rag doll. Wind whipped long strands of hair across her face, wiping away her tears. She stared at her feet, afraid to look at the kids playing on the other side of the schoolyard.

Or…

Example: *Telling: George was a disgusting slob. He played video games all day and never picked up a thing. His room was littered with trash.*

Or...

Showing: George sat in on the edge of his rumpled, unmade bed and hunched over his computer. His tiny room reeked of sweat, soiled clothes and rancid food. Empty cola cans and dirty paper plates littered the floor. A half-eaten piece of pizza, dried and curling, stained the carpet near the bed.

It's easy to tell the reader that George is a slob. However, it's far more interesting if the writer describes the conditions that allow the reader to conclude he's a slob rather than just telling the reader that he is. Describing the conditions and actions is *showing*, or "proving" the point.

Example: *Telling: Every time Bill smelled Magnolia blossoms he remembered his first love, Beth. One day, as he headed for the Language Arts Building to teach his class, he passed a magnolia tree in full bloom. Its scent brought back a flood of wonderful memories. That's when he decided to call her.*

Or...

Showing: Bill hurried toward the Language Arts building, his briefcase filled with notes for his next class. He brushed past a magnolia tree near the walk and the musty sweet odor of its plump blossoms magically scented the air and caught him off guard for a moment. He hesitated without further thought of his class and paused to pull a single petal from a bloom. He held it to his nose and breathed deeply, momentarily letting the scent carry him gently back to summers long past, where the magnolia trees outside Beth's bedroom subtly sweetened the air as they made love. At that moment, he vowed to find her.

Sensory perception plays an enormous part in every person's life and it should be in the life of your characters. They should be aware if clothes are too tight, if the sound of a mosquito is distracting, if the taste of fish lingers too long or if the air is uncomfortably hot or cold. Without these flashes of information, your characters lack depth and seem wooden.

Even more important is the way your character *feels*—the hurts, joys, hopes and fears. A story in which a character doesn't "feel" is nothing more than an incident told by an unconcerned stranger. They are like unseasoned food—easy to leave untouched.

Faking Emotion

Inexperienced writers, especially those who have difficulty dealing with raw emotion in real life, often "fake" emotion by asking questions that imply internal turmoil.

Example: *Faking Emotion.*

Helen waited nervously outside the principal's office, wondering why she had been called to the school. Had Johnny talked back? Fail to do his homework? Or was it worse... did he hurt someone again?

There is nothing wrong with occasionally asking an internal question. It's simply much stronger to allow the character act. This character, Helen, has been called to the school to meet with the principal. Surely, some of these questions will be answered in their conversation. This is a time to enhance the character by showing her nervousness and discomfort.

Example: *Describing Emotion*

Helen's hands trembled as she twisted her purse strap. No one had actually said Johnny was in trouble again, but there was no other reason for the school to have called her. She glanced around the small waiting room and tried to ignore the guilt tightened her throat and the stinging tears pushing behind her eyelids. She blinked quickly to keep from crying.

(Fast forward the story) *Helen is in the principal's office. He sits soberly a minute, a grim expression on his face, then says, "This morning Johnny choked another student. A little girl."*

Example: *Faked Emotion.*

Helen gasped and whimpered. "Choked...? Who?"

She heard the principal continue speaking but his words escaped her tormented mind. Where she had failed? How could Johnny have turned out this way? What had she done wrong?

This scene has strong potential. But pure, garden-variety *feelings* were substituted with a bunch of soap opera teaser questions. The writer hoped to reveal her torment and create tension, but questions do not allow readers to see Helen's anxiety. It is assumed, but so is tomorrow's sunrise which is not nearly as glorious as seeing it.

Remember: you are not just the writer and the director, but also *all* of the actors. No one can breathe life into them except you. Let them act!

Let's return to the emotionless scene with Helen. This is the way it might read if the writer had shown physical responses to her mental agony.

Example: *Her heart hammered at the principal's words. A strained cry escaped her throat. Suddenly engulfed in suffocating heat, she breathed deeply, fighting off nausea. She wanted to look* *up, to face him and pretend to be rational, but guilt and shame wouldn't allow it. This was all her fault. The divorce had changed Johnny. Her sweet, loving 10-year-old had turned hateful and bitter. Hot tears slipped down her cheeks and wet her tightly gripped hands.*

A general rule of thumb regarding questions is: Ask questions in dialogue; make statements in narration. That doesn't mean your character can *never* have internal questions. It means do not substitute questions for physical responses to internal struggles. Let your characters *act*.

Character Motivation

To write a successful story, your characters must be properly motivated.

There must be a logical reason for their otherwise illogical action.

For instance, if a character commits murder, his motivation for doing so must convince the reader that he believed the murder was absolutely necessary. The person he killed created a life-threatening situation for him or someone he loved, and the threat was conveyed to the reader convincingly.

Motivation is the **WHY** behind the action, and it must always be revealed.

If a man jumps off an 10-story building, everybody wonders why he was so depressed. What happened to make him want to end his life? Did no one see it coming?

The same questions apply to your character's actions. If a heroine is too frightened to open a closet door, the reader must be told why, otherwise, she will appear to be silly and totally unsympathetic.

It is easy to write about emotions is because everyone has them and although we may respond differently, we all respond. If you are unaccustomed to paying attention to your emotions, the following question may help you identify some of your responses.

How does your body respond when you're afraid?

What happens to your heart? Does it pump hard and fast?

What happens to your breathing? Do you feel breathless?

What happens to your hands? Do they get sweaty and clammy?

What about your mouth? Does it become dry?

Do you open your eyes very wide or blink rapidly?

Do you tremble and shake or become stiff and robotic?

When you try to talk, how does your voice sound? Does it get all shaky and weak or grow louder?

Example: *Miss Clark slammed the book down. Hands on her hips, she glared at the students. "All right!" she snapped, "I've had just about enough of this nonsense!"*

Did you know that Miss Clark was angry, even though there is no mention of her anger? Were her actions enough to convince you that she was angry? She might have screamed and pounded the table. She might even have been trembling. We know all of this because these are the actions and responses of someone who is angry.

Writing Exercise

Part 1 – List some of the ways your body responds when you are scared, angry, happy and sad.

Part 2 – Choose three of the situations below and write three or four sentences describing how the following characters feel and act.

1) *Adam, 22, has just robbed a house while no one was home. A mile from that house he is stopped by the police for a traffic violation. Describe his panic without resorting to words synonymous with panic. Let his actions reveal it.*

2) *Rachel, 45, has just learned that her 14-year-old daughter has been kidnapped. Show what she is feeling. Describe her actions and dialogue.*

3) *Mr. Martin, 70, is grieving because his beloved wife died. Show his grief without telling the reader he is sad. Describe his actions. What does he do and say?*

4) *Julie, age 12, is very happy. She has just learned that her parents who were divorced are getting back together. Show how she feels. Describe how she acts.*

5) *Tim, 19, has just discovered that someone slashed his tires and he has no money to replace them. Show his words and actions without saying he was furious, mad, angry, etc.*

Making Your Characters Believable

Believable characters respond to life in the same way that real people respond. Everyone's mood changes from time to time, and your character will experience different moods throughout your story. When that happens, the change will cast everything in a differently light. It will affect every aspect of the situation and influence every action and response.

Example: Sam, age 14, has just arrived home from school. He's happy because his report card is filled with A's and B's. He's never received such good grades.

The front door was stuck again. Sam leaned against it and nudged it open. Inside, he looked around at the empty living room. The old couch invited him to sit awhile. The pictures of his grandparents on the mantle smiled down at him as if they were proud of the report card in his pocket. Moving to the window, he opened the blinds and let the sun stream in, brightening the room. This is a good house, he thought. I can't wait for Mom and Dad to get home.

Example: Sam, age 14, just arrived home from school. He's depressed and angry about his report card. It's filled with all D's and F's.

The front door was stuck again. Furious, Sam slammed his body against it. It crashed open. Inside, he stared at the empty living room. The old couch looked dirty and uncomfortable. The pictures of his grandparents on the mantle seemed to mock him. He could practically hear them saying, "We're so disappointed, Sam." Moving to the window, Sam closed the blinds even tighter. He wanted to disappear into the darkness of this ugly, old house, and never have to face his parents again

As you can see, the two scenes are exactly alike, except for the character's mood. When Sam's mood changed, everything else seemed to change.

Creating Memorable Characters

The best characters are those that readers remember forever. And one of the ways to create memorable characters is to make them *different*. Fortunately, there are two ways to do that. The first is to make them physically different, such as *Superman* or *The Ugly Duckling*. The second is to make them mentally or emotionally different. Characters who are mentally or emotionally different do not think and act like everyone else. Consequently, we love them or hate them more than other characters.

The Little Engine That Could was probably one of the first stories you ever heard or read. Do you remember how strongly you felt when you heard it? Children have loved it since the day it was written because *The Little Engine That Could* was mentally and emotionally *different*. He refused to quit, and readers love a character that is determined and *different*.

Think about your real life heroes and favorite fictional characters for a moment and you'll see that the ones you like best are always different. Sometimes the difference is physical and other times it's mental or emotional.

Making the Unbelievable Believable

If you want to create a super hero, such as Superman, you must explain how your character came to have supernatural powers, and you must do it in the first part of the story. Even if your reason is not too believable, the readers will accept it if you present it in the beginning of the story. If you do not, the readers will think *you* are crazy for expecting them to believe that such a super person exists.

Example: *Jan stared at the door, afraid to knock. She had to warn Mrs. Scott to stay away from Hampton Street tomorrow. She couldn't go near it... not if she wanted to stay alive. But how would she tell her without sounding like a crazy person? Even if she told her the truth—that every* *time she put on the sunglasses she found in the alley, she could see the future—Mrs. Scott wouldn't believe her. Who would? Jan could hardly believe it herself.*

Writing Exercise

Write an opening paragraph about a character that is able to make dead plants come alive and grow again. Show the character using this super power and explain how s/he came to have it.

Different Thoughts and Emotions

When creating a character who thinks differently than others, it is not so necessary to explain how or why. The character's words and actions will convince the reader that he or she is not only different, but good or bad.

In *The Christmas Carol* by Charles Dickens, the character, Scrooge, is definitely different. He is meaner and more heartless than most people. This doesn't have to be explained because everyone knows what it is to feel mean and heartless. Everyone has experienced that feeling at one time or another.

Writing Exercise

Part 1

Your character is able to turn him/herself into many different things, such as a tree, a thunderstorm, or an ant. First, explain how s/he is able to do this and show the character using this power for good or evil.

Part 2

Your character is terrified of cats. Show your character in a scene with a cat then show the reader why s/he is terrified. You may do this by having the character remember a terrible incident with a cat or by having someone else explain your character's strange behavior.

Part 3

Your character, a poor student, is suddenly "gifted." Explain how this happened.

Consistency

Characters are sometimes put into situations that cause them to change, to grow, or to learn life lessons that have somehow escaped them prior to the opening of the story. Usually, in a short time frame, they face many problems and conflicts, and must deal with external and internal struggles. However, the change within the fictional character must be as consistent and realistic as it is with real people.

For instance, a man who hates mashed potatoes, rock music, and a particular ethnic group in the beginning of a story will also hate them in the middle and end of the story *unless* something happens *during the story* to prompt a change of heart. But, be careful. Changes take time and are long in coming, just as they are in real life. What we love or despise today, we will love and despise tomorrow unless something happens to dramatically change our attitude. Don't forget this. If your character changes without proper motivation, he becomes less believable and the reader may lose interest in him. Be consistent.

Quirks

Quirks, or peculiar traits, generally make people interesting. A man who eats raw meat and sleeps on the floor is dramatically more interesting than a man who eats cooked meat and sleeps in a bed. Don't be afraid to give your characters a "quirk," yet don't overdo it, either.

"But," you protest, "a man who eats raw meat and sleeps on the floor is not very believable."

Well, neither was the Superman until the creator explained how he got his super power. Once explained, no one objects, but the explaining must come at the beginning of the story, never at the end. Only the unexplained becomes a worrisome monster that will kill your story.

Physical Environment

Successful writers know that their character's environment is as important as his thoughts, actions, and words. Without taking time to create scene details that make the picture come alive, your character will seem to be moving in a void. Readers can't identify with what's not there. However, this does not mean you must write lengthy passages describing a single room. A few carefully constructed lines can have a strong emotional impact.

Example: Claire lounged on the couch, her eyes fastened on the daytime drama blaring from the TV, a half-knitted sweater draped on the floor beside her. Two empty beer cans and a half-eaten bag of potato chips littered the table. The chair on the opposite wall seemed to sag beneath the load of dirty clothes piled ready for washing, but apparently forgotten. Dishes stacked three and four deep, bearing the remains of several meals, cluttered the small apartment's kitchen counter, their contents dried and curling around the edges.

From the above description, it might appear that Claire is a terrible housekeeper. But she could be an invalid, a lonely senile old lady or suffering from the loss of a loved one. No mention was made of Claire except that she lounged on the couch, yet a strong impression of her environment is left in the reader's mind.

Example: *Claire lounged on the couch. A half-knitted sweater, neatly folded, lay on the floor at her feet while she watched the daytime drama blaring from the TV. A fresh bouquet of flowers brightened the table beside her. The chair on the opposite wall displayed her latest crocheted doilies on both arms, and the kitchen counter gleamed in the bright afternoon sunlight.*

From this description, it appears that Claire is a conscientious housekeeper who has momentarily put down her knitting to enjoy a favorite daytime TV show. Still, she might have been visiting someone not in the room at that moment. No mention was made of Clair except that she lounged on the couch.

Had I said only that she lounged on the couch and not added a few sentences to describe the apartment, the reader would have felt a sense of loss and been forced to create an image of Clair and the apartment. Thus, the description of Claire's apartment told us a great deal about her, even though little mention was made of Claire.

Descriptive detail of a character's environment is as necessary to a story as the background in a painting.

For instance, a picture of a sad-eyed little puppy may be adorable, yet it doesn't evoke nearly the emotion of a sad-eyed little puppy sitting beside an overturned trashcan in a dark alley. To change the picture again, simply by changing the background detail, imagine the same sad-eyed puppy sitting under a wealthy family's dinner table. Emotions change when the scene changes.

So, like an artist, you must detail the setting or environment of your characters in order to evoke the emotional response you want.

Environment Props

You may also use various props from the environment to help describe your character. Let the sun, wind, rain, and other objects in the room help define them.

Example: As Sally leaned against the open door, a sudden gust of wind rushed in. Her long red hair fanned about her face and danced in the lingering breeze. Her pale green summer dress swirled about her knees but she didn't seem to notice. "That's nice," she said, lifting her face to air. "I'm love summer."

Or...

Example: Tommy squatted in front of the TV, looking up only occasionally as he played with the kitten. His tee shirt and cut-offs were almost as dirty as his feet.

In the first example, the doorway where Sally leaned *and* the wind are used to help describe her character. Leaning shows that she is either tired or relaxed. Her response to the wind tells us she likes it. Using the wind to fan her hair about her face is a way to describe her hair without saying something dull, such as: *Sally had long, red hair.*

In the second example, the TV is an environmental prop. It helps to show Tommy as an average kid. What he is doing and what he is wearing also tell us that he's an ordinary kid. Using the TV and kitten help the reader to see more of Tommy than just his clothes. These things also tell us what Tommy enjoys doing.

Writing Exercise

Describe the following characters. Use details of the environment to reveal something about them.

A young girl or boy caught in a rainstorm

An elderly man or woman getting off a bus

A father or mother in a rush to leave for work

DIALOGUE

Dialogue is probably the most interesting element of a story because it can pass enormous amounts of information about the character and the plot. Not only is it an effective way for the reader to see a character's thoughts and the emotion behind those thoughts, it also establishes intelligence, background, education and personality.

However, there are only TWO reasons for using dialogue in a story: 1) to strengthen the character, and 2) to advance the plot. No matter how clever you think a line is, if it does not fulfill one of these two purposes, it should be stricken. Unnecessary dialogue slows the story, often misleads the reader, and frequently kills suspense.

Real people have different speech patterns, and so should your characters. Let some speak with short, snappy sentences while others speak slowly in long, drawn out sentences. Still others will add unnecessary details to everything they say and need to be interrupted and forced to their point.

Different dialogue patterns add personality and flavor a story, and if carefully written, will instantly identify the speakers.

Blend Dialogue with Narration and Action

Dialogue can be strong enough to stand alone, but for the most part, it is best to blend it with narration and action. Stagnant blocks of dialogue tend to be awkward, whereas a good mixture of dialogue, narration, and action creates exciting scenes and keeps the reader's mind stimulated.

There are no hard and fast rules about how long a speaker may talk, but it's good to keep dialogue short and allow another character to speak. In normal conversations, there is a continual exchange, even if one person merely grunts or gestures to indicate he understands the speaker's point.

An exception is if one person is deliberately lecturing another. But, even then it only takes a few sentences for the reader to get the message.

Example: *"Lecture" dialogue: Helen shook her drink slowly, watching the golden scotch swirl around the ice cubes.*

"I came down to the office today, Bill. You weren't there. Neither was Myrna. I'm not implying anything, dear, there's no need to." Her smile was full of contempt. "No, there's no need to imply anything because, you see, I saw you—the two of you coming out of a restaurant across the street. What have you got to say for yourself?"

Well, the reader got the point and presumably so did Bill, but it would have been more interesting if there had been an exchange of dialogue between characters. The exchange lets us see the whole picture—how the other person is responding.

Example*: "I was by the office today, Bill."*

"So?"

"And Myrna wasn't there."

"So?"

"And neither were you."

Bill turned slowly from the window to face her. "And you're implying that we were together, right?"

"I'm not implying anything, dear. There's no need to." She shook her drink slowly, a cunning smile twisting her mouth.

"Good. In that case, we'll drop the subject." He turned back to stare out the window again.

Helen strode across the room angrily and grabbed his arm. "I saw you with her! Coming out of the restaurant across the street!"

As you can see, the lines are short and the dialogue furthers the plot and strengthens the characters.

There are two scenes in particular where dialogue needs to be held to a minimum: love scenes and fight scenes (arguments). When over-written, both become weak and often humorous. Be extremely selective with dialogue or it will betray you and destroy the scene.

One of the best ways to study dialogue is to watch TV and movies. Notice that the camera focuses on the speaker, who rarely speaks more than a few seconds—a line or two. The camera catches the speaker's expression, or acting. The camera then switches the next speaker, for the same reason—to catch the expression/response—*unless* another character's expression/response is more important to the story.

What the camera reveals in a movie, a novelist must describe with words. The writer becomes the camera, describing the squints, grimaces; laughter and mockery of each character, *and* must write the dialogue as well.

Writing "Natural Dialogue"

New writers sometimes have a difficult time with dialogue because they forget that it's necessary to use contractions, incomplete sentences, repetitive phrases, and even poor grammar in order to make their fictional characters sound natural. For instance, if a character is uneducated, his/her dialogue should reflect it. If the character is a schoolteacher, his/her dialogue should reflect that.

A line such as, "I cannot abide this one more day" would be hilarious if given to a burly truck driver who would more than likely say, "Screw this!"

One of the surest ways to discover unnatural sounding dialogue is to read it aloud or have someone else read it to you while you listen, critique it, and make notes.

Unless you are writing about a pretentious character who constantly struggles to impress everyone, then write dialogue that represents your character and his/her attitudes.

As stated earlier: Dialogue serves two, and only two, purposes: 1) to advance the plot, and 2) enhance the character.

Example: *Unnatural Dialogue*

"Oh, dear, I think you might need to stop the car. I'm about to lose my lunch."

Or...

(Natural or realistic dialogue)

"Stop the car! I'm gonna throw up!"

Simply allow your characters to use everyday words and phrases.

An exception to the rule is dialects. These, you do not want to write realistically because they are difficult to read and the last thing you want is to make your reader stumble. "Stumbles" are distractions that often make readers want to set the book aside

Example: *WRONG way to handle dialects:*

"Iffin I wuz to take a walk, a-hikin' through them thar hills, I reckon you'unzes ud hafta foller me, don'tcha thank?"

Instead, merely flavor the dialogue so that the reader gets the point without having to trip and stumble.

"If I was to take a walk through them there hills, I reckon you'd have to foller me, don'cha think?"

In this example, instead of many colloquialisms to stumble through, there are only a few, and it reads much more smoothly while still conveying the same impression and message.

Taglines

Taglines are the lines tagged onto dialogue to identify the speaker. They should be eliminated wherever possible. Characters and their particular speech patterns should be strong enough to indicate who is speaking. However, if two characters are similar or there is a long passage of dialogue exchange so that there might be confusion without the taglines, then use them.

An occasional "he said" or "she said" is sufficient and even necessary at times. But, vary the pattern. Don't have repetitive "he said" after each line of dialogue. Break up the attributives and the sentences so that the interruptions flow naturally.

Example: *Repetitive taglines*

"Well, what are we going to do now?" he asked.

"I don't know," she said.

"Maybe we could drop the body in the lake," he said.

"But it might float," she said.

Improve tagline placement by inserting them into the lines of dialogue at natural pausing points.

Example:

"Well," he said, "what are we going to do now?"

"I don't know."

"Maybe," he said thoughtfully, "we could drop the body in the lake."

She looked at him skeptically. "Won't it float?"

A still better way is to tag the speaker with an action line. Action lines are rarely repetitive or boring.

Example:

Harry paced the cabin floor. "What are we going to do now?"

"I don't know." She watched him intently.

"Maybe," he paused as he studied the darkness outside. "Maybe we could drop the body in the lake."

She gaped incredulously at him. "Won't it float?"

Avoid forced adjectives that are intended to connote action, but instead turn an otherwise good piece of writing into an obviously amateurish attempt.

Example:

"Help me!" she called PLEADINGLY.

It is much stronger to say: *"Help me!" she pleaded.*

"Please don't go!" he cried SADLY. If he's crying, the reader knows he's sad.

Don't be redundant. It will not make the dialogue stronger, only longer... and a bit silly.

Action

No story survives without action. Action creates interest. Without it, writers write essays and articles. No piece of fiction will survive without action.

To create a sense of action, use descriptive, colorful verbs. Instead of saying "He sat down," describe *how* he sat: "He plopped down." "He dropped down," "He eased down," etc. Draw a mental picture with an action word.

Also, you can write more dynamically if you use the active voice as much as possible. For instance, the sentence "The story had been written by me" becomes stronger and more direct when you change it to "I wrote the story."

Frequently, beginning writers get so caught up in their own brilliance as they narrate the story, they forget to let characters act. Yet, healthy people move when they stand, sit and talk. They fidget, squirm, pace, or just pick lint off their clothes. Don't forget to give your character physical actions while he's talking, waiting in a room, thinking, etc. If he does nothing more than sigh, then at least have him sigh now and then so the reader knows he didn't die.

Show action, don't tell it

Generally, new writers paraphrase the action instead of describing it so the reader can see it. The difference is critical if you hope to sell the story. For instance, it's not uncommon to destroy a fight scene by "telling" (paraphrasing) the action.

Example: Helen screamed at Bill that he was a no-good woman-chasing rat and he yelled back that she was nothing to brag about. Furious, Helen threw a vase at him and missed. It shattered the window instead, and Bill, although still mad, couldn't keep from laughing.

It would have been much better to have described (shown) the action.

Example: Helen glared and clenched her fists: "You no-good woman-chasing rat!"

Bill whirled to face her. "Me? You're calling me names?" He raised his voice dramatically and pointed an accusing finger. "I don't think you'd win any prizes for fidelity, sweetheart!" He turned and bolted for the door.

"You!" Helen screamed, "I'll kill you!" She grabbed a vase and hurled it at him. It missed his head by inches and crashed into the window. Glass shattered in an earsplitting crescendo.

Stunned at first, Bill stopped. He looked back uncertainly then burst out laughing. "You fool! You poor, dimwitted fool!"

Generally speaking, it takes more effort, thought and words to "show" action, but the results are worth it, especially if you have hopes of selling the story.

To sum up, don't tell—or paraphrase—the action, describe it. SHOW IT!

Creating a sense of action

A potentially great action scene can be ruined if the writer is unaware that the very length of a sentence plays a critical role in strengthening or weakening the scene. Suspense and action is enhanced through the use of short, snappy sentences. Long sentences with several "ing" words slow the action and tend to kill suspense. Conversely, short sentences and strong active verbs negatively affect passages intended to create a feeling peace and well-being.

Example: "She screamed. Ran. Dived into the lake," conveys a sense of spontaneous action more than "She screamed and ran and dived into the lake."

However, if a character is exhausted and finally able to rest, it helps to build a feeling of fatigue and/or peace by using longer sentences. (Read page 25 again.)

Flashbacks and Transitions

The flashback—the moment when the writer suddenly takes the reader back in time—can be a handy tool for the experienced writer, but that is generally because the experienced writer has learned to avoid it. A successful flashback is one that's unavoidable; there is simply no other way to tell the story. However, it is almost always best to structure a story so that the action stays in the present. Sometimes this means telling the backstory first and flashing forward. .

When an unavoidable flashback situation arises, then the "bridge" or transition lines used to transport the reader smoothly from one time period to another is critical. It must be done with as little interruption as possible and as briefly as practicable in order to avoid disturbing the continuity of the story.

Example: POOR flashback transition (Bill is starting his vacation):

Bill suddenly remembered his grandmother. She used to bake cookies and set them on the table for anyone who wanted one.

As Bill thought about this, he remembered his old dog, Pooch, and how he used to slip up from under the table and steal half a dozen cookies before grandma got wise.

And thinking about Pooch reminded him of when he used to fish in the murky pond down on the south end of the farm...and so forth until the transition becomes so labored with short recollections that the reader becomes impatient.

If you must go, GO! And hurry.

Example: Bill stared at the endless line of traffic ahead of him. It would be good to see his grandparents and the farm again. If he could just relax as he had as a boy... sit by the pond and not have a care in the world.

"Bill. Come here!" His grandmother's cheery call carried across the years. "Bill, I baked some cookies."

Tearing across the field through long rows of corn, dust rising from his feet and a strap flying loose from his coveralls, he dashed for the house.

Transport the reader quickly and smoothly from one time period to the next and place them directly in the middle of the action.

When your reader has been smoothly taken back in time several times and the plot no longer depends on the information divulged in these flashbacks, it is permissible to simply leave several spaces in your copy to indicate a break, and to begin the flashback scene. This technique, however, cannot be employed unless the reader has been thoroughly familiarized with all your characters in the past. In other words, you can't jump back 10 to 50 years and begin action around characters not yet identified without totally confusing, and losing, your reader.

Also, never interrupt an action scene with flashback. The reader will likely want to strangle you.

Example: *Richard ran until he thought his heart would burst. He glanced back several times to see if they were still following him. He finally ducked between two buildings. The intense darkness blacked out the end of the alley, reminding him of when he used to try to slip home in the dark. His 12-year-old clumsiness always betrayed him. Invariably, he would trip over something and...*

It sounds ridiculous that anyone would leave an exciting chase scene to flashback to a less exciting time, but it happens. Simply put, don't do it.

Perhaps the most tiresome of all transitions are those that involve moving your character physically from one room to another.

Example: *(Awkward transition)*

"I don't care if I ever see you again!" Helen yelled as she bolted out of the room. She slammed the door, hurried down the hall, punched the elevator button and waited. It seemed an eternity before it got there and when it did, she entered, punched the button to the garage and descended.

Jabbing the key into the ignition, she pulled out of the stall, backed up and headed out of the building. On Fourth Street, she pulled to the curb and parked.

She would show him this time. The Lantern Bar. That's where she'd go. Nothing would irritate him more.

The stale air rushed out as she walked in...

Such unnecessary details are boring and quickly kill interest. The reader doesn't care about the actual physical maneuvering of your characters as long as you get them where they're supposed to be for the next scene.

Example: *"I don't care if I ever see you again!" Helen yelled as she bolted out of the room. Determined to hurt him as much as she could, she deliberately drove to the Lantern Bar. Nothing would sting worse than for him to find her at the Lantern!*

The stale air rushed out as she walked in...

Keep in mind at all times that your readers want action, not monotonous details of walking, opening doors, riding buses, cars, etc.

AFTER WRITING

Editing

To become a successful writer, you must be willing to do the tedious but necessary job of editing—strengthening the weak spots, pruning or cutting "too wordy" passages, re-writing entire chapters, and reviewing each word and phrase. There is no other way to create a marketable piece. Editing also involves checking the details of the story for accuracy, the characters for believability and consistency, and the plot for soundness.

Most successful authors prefer to write a story from beginning to end and *then* edit so that they don't disturb the continuity of the story.

To edit a single chapter or scene and consider it "finished" before the whole story or book is completed is likely to cause big problems later. First, the natural flow may be interrupted, and perhaps even more frustrating, halfway through you may decide to change the story somewhat. In order to do this, a complete re-working of the entire story will be required, especially if the change involves the plot. The story will need restructuring from beginning to end, and all of the effort that went into your edited chapter will have been wasted.

After the first draft of your story is completed, read it again for weaknesses in both characters and plot. When this has been done and necessary notes and changes made, read the entire story again (regardless of whether it's 10 or 500 pages) and the second time through, check for all weak verbs, lackluster sentences, and polish your characters until each one performs exactly as you want. In other words, check every word of every line to make sure it is the word that says exactly what you want to say, the way you want to say it.

Generally, a piece should be completely "gone over" four or five times before considering it finished—and certainly before submitting it anywhere. Even then, it's wise to give it to proofreader to check for mistakes. Find a retired English teacher to proof your work if you can or spend the money to hire a professional proofreader. It will save you regrets and embarrassment in the long run because it's almost impossible to proof your own work. You know what you meant to say and the chances are that you will read what you meant to say instead of what you actually wrote.

Joe Blow   Approx. 1,000 words
1000 Something Block
Somewhere, State, Zip Code
joeblow@blowhard.com
www.blowhard.net

SETTING UP A MANUSCRIPT

by

Joe Blow

The first page of every manuscript submitted to a traditional publisher should look like this page. Name and contact numbers in the upper left corner, the word count in the upper right.

Drop down several spaces before typing the title. If your story is accepted, this space is used by the editors to give instructions for printing.

Under the title, type your name, then drop down two lines and begin your story. Each succeeding page should include your name and the page number. On the bottom of the last page, you may type "the end," although that should be fairly obvious.

If submitting a hard copy, enclose a stamped, self-addressed envelope so that your manuscript can be returned if rejected.

However, some publishers no longer return manuscripts, and state that on their websites.

Jot down the date that you mail the manuscript then forget that particular story. Begin working on another. If you just sit and wait to see if your work is accepted, time will drag unmercifully.

Most magazines take three to six weeks to reply, some as long as 90 days. Many book publishers take four to six months to respond, and some never do. For all you know, it was dumped, unread.

If you have not heard from the publisher after three months, drop a note and politely ask if your manuscript was received. If there is no reply within a month, ask again. However, if there was no reply to the first request, the second one may not be answered either. All that you can do is wait and get busy writing another story.

Online publishers are quicker to respond and far more accepting of new authors. If you have edited and polished your work until you are convinced it is the best you can do, you can also self-publish on several different sites. If you choose to do that, the next step is the same as it would be if you were dealing with a traditional publisher: get busy writing your next novel or story *and* learn how to promote the book you have posted online. Let people know your book is available.

There are dozens of online sites that promote books and writers. Investigate them and choose the one you can afford and that you believe is best for you.

Query Letters

As you approach the end of your manuscript, stop for a day or two and draft a solid query letter. There are many books today, digital and paper, which detail what is expected of a good query letter. It's important to query publishers before submitting. Most traditional publishers do not read unsolicited manuscripts, but queries are generally answered. If your story idea excites them, they will ask to see a chapter or perhaps the whole manuscript. If that happens—rejoice!

Online publishers are usually quicker to respond and there are many online sites to post your book digitally. Of course, they will take a percentage of each sale, but so do the traditional publishers.

To publish an e-Book, simply read the submission guidelines.

SALES & REJECTIONS
(The "highs" and "lows" of writing)

Rejection slips are almost as inevitable to as death and taxes. Editors receive countless numbers of stories to review every day. Many are rejected immediately because they don't meet the magazine's format or publisher's current needs. Who can blame a publisher of thriller novels for quickly rejecting a cookbook from a writer too lazy to do a little research?

Yes, sometimes an editor's judgment is flawed. They're human, too. We've all read about a best-selling book that was rejected 10 or 15 times before a publisher decided to take a chance on it?

I know a short story writer who submitted and re-submitted her stories until the cost of the postage was greater than what she could get for the story if it sold. With one story, she determined she could send it out 13 times. However, she could only find 12 possible markets. So after she had been rejected by the 12th, she sent it back to the first editor that rejected it—and this time, sold it!

Go figure. Perhaps the first time it was rejected the editor had been in a fender-bender and was in no mood to accept anything. Or maybe the second time it arrived a scheduled piece wasn't finished and the magazine had two pages to fill. There is no way to know, but she certainly celebrated for having sent it out the 13th time.

It is always discouraging to be rejected, but don't give up. Keep writing, editing and submitting your work. If you follow the suggestions at the beginning of this book, you will have analyzed the market before you started writing, and your story will be written to meet the current needs of specific magazines or publishers. Consequently, your chance of selling the piece will be greatly enhanced.

If your story is rejected repeatedly, then perhaps, it has flaws that need correcting. However, if your story is relatively fresh (written within the past six months), you may not have the objectivity needed to catch the errors or weaknesses. So put it away for six months and then re-read it. By then, you will probably have "fresh eyes" and be better able to see how the story can be revised and strengthened.

If you doubt your story will actually be read by an editor, resist the urge to behave like an immature, frustrated child. Some writers are so skeptical, they actually turn a page upside down, or use a speck of glue on a couple of pages to see if the manuscript comes back with the pages separated and right side up.

This not only wastes time, but often prejudices the editor against your work before he even reads it. Some editors become so aggravated by this tactic that they say they deliberately turn pages upside down after they've read them and are especially careful not to unstick any glued pages.

If you are serious about becoming a writer, you must realize that you have embarked on a long and difficult, but exciting journey. You are headed for a destination that you may not reach for a long time. But eventually, when you sell your first story, you will truly understand that it was worth all the effort and frustration. The feeling of pride, accomplishment, and confidence that you experience is far more exhilarating than you ever imagined.

You are a writer - a published author! Congratulations! Go celebrate!

Othello Bach

Othello is a multi-genre author of numerous books, which range in scope and variety from suspense novels to children's books to non-fiction "How-to" books. Her memoir "Cry into the Wind," chronicles an abusive childhood, including 11 years in an orphanage.

Although a non-reader until the eighth grade, she wrote and sold her first novel to Avon Books when she was 22.

Othello often composes music and lyrics to accompany her children's stories, and celebrities Joel Grey, Tammy Grimes and Sandy Duncan have recorded her books and songs.

She is a motivational speaker who loves to share "the tools" that helped her overcome an abusive past.

Othello welcomes all reader questions and comments, email her at othellobach@comcast.net.

www.amazon.com/author/othellobach
www.othellobach.com
www.whoeverheardofafird.com
http://ramblingsbyothello.wordpress.com/feed/
http://www.twitter.com/OthelloBach
http://www.amazon.com/dp/B00FPXDCWA

www.ingramcontent.com/pod-product-compliance
Lightning Source LLC
Chambersburg PA
CBHW030518290526
45786CB00004B/1512